ELIMINATION

DIET FOR ADHD

Unlocking Focus and Wellness with the Ultimate Elimination Diet Manual.

GLEN N. QUIRK

TABLE OF CONTENT

Chapter 6 171

Introduction

In a quiet suburban neighborhood, young James lived with a bright and creative spirit. However, he faced a unique challenge—Attention Deficit Hyperactivity Disorder (ADHD). James struggled with concentration, often finding it hard to focus or sit still, which impacted his performance at school.

His parents, Sarah and Mark, were determined to find a solution. After extensive research and advice from healthcare professionals, they decided to make significant changes to James's diet.

Guided by a registered dietitian, they overhauled James's diet. Sugary cereals and processed snacks were replaced with whole grains, fruits, and vegetables. Soda was swapped for water, and fast food was replaced with home-cooked meals featuring lean proteins, healthy fats, and a variety of colorful fruits and vegetables.

As weeks passed, James exhibited improved focus and less impulsivity. He started completing homework without constant redirection, and his grades improved. Cooking with his mother became a bonding experience, and it brought their family closer.

In addition to the dietary changes, James embraced physical activity. He took up swimming and cycling, channeling his energy in a positive way and enhancing his focus.

James learned to manage his ADHD with the right diet, the support of his family, and his determination. While he still had moments of restlessness and distraction, he had developed the tools to cope with them, allowing his true potential to shine through.

James's story inspired many, a testament to the remarkable change that can occur when one embraces the power of a balanced, nutritious diet. It served as a reminder that, with the right tools and support, anyone can overcome the challenges they face and thrive.

Understanding ADHD and Diet

ADHD is a neurodevelopmental condition that impacts individuals of all ages and is distinguished by recurrent episodes of hyperactivity, impulsivity, and inattention. There is increasing interest in the importance of nutrition as an adjunctive strategy to control ADHD symptoms, even if behavioral therapy and, in certain situations, medication are the main methods of managing ADHD.

We will examine the following important components in this section:

Describe ADHD

ADHD is a complicated disorder with several facets that can greatly affect a person's day-to-day functioning. *Let's examine the main characteristics of ADHD in order to comprehend its ramifications more fully:*

A. Inattention: People with ADHD frequently have trouble focusing, paying attention to details, and finishing tasks. They might routinely misplace things, forget appointments, and commit thoughtless errors at work or school.

B. Hyperactivity: This condition is characterized by a continual need to move and restlessness. It can be difficult for someone with ADHD to remain motionless, to stop other people in mid-sentence, or to act impulsively.

C. Impulsivity: The act of behaving without considering the repercussions is referred to as impulsivity. This may result in unsafe actions, trouble waiting one's time, and a lot of interruptions.

It is noteworthy that individuals with ADHD exhibit varying degrees of severity and mix of symptoms, indicating that the condition is not universally present. A formal diagnosis usually entails a thorough evaluation by a licensed healthcare provider, like a psychiatrist or psychologist.

Diet's Function in Managing ADHD

When it comes to managing the symptoms of ADHD, diet is very important. Although nutrition cannot treat ADHD on its own, it can affect the severity of symptoms and general wellbeing. This is how managing ADHD and food interact:

A. dietary shortages: Studies indicate that people with ADHD may be more vulnerable to iron, zinc, magnesium, and omega-3 fatty acids, among other dietary shortages. These nutrients can affect mood and attention and are necessary for brain function.

B. Blood Sugar Levels: Variations in blood sugar levels can impact one's capacity for focus and vigor. Blood sugar fluctuations brought on by diets heavy in processed foods and refined sugars may exacerbate symptoms of ADHD.

C. Artificial food additives and preservatives: (e.g., food dyes, artificial sweeteners) and their possible association with symptoms of ADHD have been investigated in a few research, especially that involving youngsters. There's conflicting evidence, but some people might be allergic to certain drugs.

Why Take Into Account a Dietary Elimination?

Identifying and eliminating possible trigger foods that could exacerbate symptoms of ADHD is the goal of an elimination diet. This is why it may be advantageous to think about going on an elimination diet:

A. Tailored Approach: Metabolic Syndrome is not a universally applicable disorder, and people may exhibit distinct dietary sensitivity issues. A customized method of determining and resolving dietary triggers that are unique to a person's needs can be achieved through an elimination diet.

B. Reducing Inflammation: Certain diets can make the body more prone to inflammation, which can have an impact on how the brain and metabolism work. It may be possible to lessen ADHD symptoms by removing possible inflammatory triggers.

C. Non-Pharmacological Approach: An elimination diet offers an alternative to medication for managing ADHD symptoms for individuals who prefer non-pharmacological approaches or are looking for supplementary techniques.

We will go into the specifics of putting an exclusion diet for ADHD into practice in the following chapters of this book, including how to recognize trigger foods, organize meals, and track your progress. Remember that although nutrition can be a useful tool in the management of ADHD, it works best when included in a full treatment plan that also includes behavioral therapy and, if required, medication therapies.

Chapter 1

What is an elimination diet?

An elimination diet is a targeted dietary approach that aims to identify and eliminate particular foods or food groups that may cause negative reactions in an individual. It entails removing suspected allergenic or problematic foods from one's diet for a short period of time and then gradually reintroducing them to determine the cause of symptoms. *This section will discuss the essential components associated with the idea of an elimination diet:*

Foundational Ideas and Concepts

Several key ideas form the foundation of an elimination diet:

Systematic Exclusion: The main idea is to cut off food groups or products that may act as triggers for a predetermined amount of time, usually a few weeks to many months.

Gradual Reintroduction: Following the elimination stage, foods are reintroduced one at a time under carefully monitored conditions to track any negative reactions.

Documentation: It entails keeping a thorough food journal to record dietary modifications, symptoms, and progress during the phases of reintroduction and elimination.

Distinct Methodologies

Elimination diets come in a variety of forms, each suited to a particular objective or set of circumstances. Common strategies consist of:

Standard Elimination Diet: An all-encompassing strategy that concentrates on cutting out common allergic foods like eggs, dairy, gluten, soy, and nuts.

FODMAP Elimination Diet: This diet targets fermentable carbohydrates that can cause digestive pain in an effort to relieve symptoms of irritable bowel syndrome (IBS).

Elimination of Specific Allergens: Addresses recognized allergens such peanuts, tree nuts, shellfish, and other particular food allergies.

Anti-Inflammatory Diet: The anti-inflammatory diet eliminates meals high in sugar, processed fats, and processed additives in an effort to lessen inflammation in the body.

Advantages and Possible Results

Beyond the primary objective of identifying trigger foods, elimination diets provide the following possible advantages and results:

Enhanced Attention and Focus

When trigger foods are cut from their diet, many people report increases in focus and attention. This is especially important for people who have disorders like ADHD or problems with their sense of smell, as food can affect how well their minds work.

Stabilization of Behavior and Mood

Modifications in diet can have a significant impact on behavior and mood. Reducing irritability, mood swings, and impulsivity might result from cutting out foods that cause negative reactions, especially in kids and adults with ADHD or mood disorders.

Elimination diets can help with broader health issues in addition to treating particular symptoms:

Digestive Health: You can reduce stomach discomfort including bloating, gas, and diarrhea by recognizing and eliminating trigger foods.

Skin Health: Removing specific foods from the diet may help those with skin issues like eczema or acne.

Allergy Management: Handling food allergies is essential to avoiding serious allergic responses and anaphylaxis.

Weight Loss and Weight Management: Some individuals discover that cutting out specific foods aids in weight loss and weight management.

Autoimmune disorders: By lowering inflammation, elimination diets can be a useful component of a holistic management strategy for autoimmune disorders.

We will go into greater detail about the ins and outs of implementing an elimination diet in the upcoming chapters, covering topics like as meal planning, technique selection, and progress tracking to help you reach your goals.

Chapter 2

Getting Ready for Your Diet of Elimination

Careful planning is necessary before starting an elimination diet to treat ADHD. This will guarantee that the journey is fruitful and successful. This stage includes a number of important components:

Evaluating Symptoms of ADHD

The first step in getting ready for an elimination diet is to understand the type and intensity of symptoms associated with ADHD. This evaluation entails:

Self-Reflection: People with ADHD or those who provide care for them should consider the particular symptoms that they or a loved one are experiencing. Keep track of the symptoms' effects on day-to-day functioning and their peak times.

Objective Observation: To obtain an objective viewpoint on ADHD symptoms, ask instructors, family members, or coworkers for their opinions. This can offer insightful information about how interactions and tasks in diverse contexts are impacted by ADHD.

Recognizing Triggers

One of the most important parts of getting ready for an elimination diet is figuring out what foods can trigger it. Remember the following:

Normal Culprits: Look at typical dietary triggers for ADHD, including as sugar, artificial coloring, artificial additives, and certain foods that cause allergies (such gluten or dairy).

Personal Observation: Keep an eye out for any trends in the worsening of symptoms after consuming particular foods. This can aid in reducing the number of possible trigger meals.

Using systematic symptom monitoring to track symptoms can help you better understand how nutrition affects symptoms of ADHD. ***Make use of a monitoring app or notebook to:***

Note Daily Observations: Keep a thorough journal of your meals, snacks, and any adjustments you notice to your symptoms of ADHD.

Take note Date and Time: Note the onset and duration of symptoms so that you can associate them with particular meals or snacks.

Consultation with medical specialists

Working together with medical experts is essential to guaranteeing your elimination diet's efficacy and safety. Consult any of the following specialists:

Nutritional Assessment: During the elimination phase, a qualified dietitian or nutritionist can evaluate your existing diet for any nutritional inadequacies and provide advice on how to keep a balanced diet.

Meal Planning: To make sure you satisfy your dietary requirements while avoiding trigger foods, they can assist you in creating wholesome, elimination-friendly meal plans.

Medical Evaluation: To verify the diagnosis of ADHD and rule out any underlying medical illnesses that can resemble symptoms of ADHD, consult a doctor or psychiatrist.

Medication Management: Talk about any modifications or concerns that might be required throughout the elimination diet if medication is a component of your ADHD treatment plan.

Clearly Determining Expectations and Goals

To effectively manage the psychological and practical components of the elimination diet, it is imperative to have well-defined objectives and expectations.

A. Practical Results

Recognize the Limitations: The degree of recovery varies from person to person, and an exclusion diet may not be able to completely remove all symptoms of ADHD.

Establish Specific Objectives: Ascertain the precise enhancements you aspire to get, such enhanced concentration, less impulsiveness, or elevated emotional state.

B. Schedule and Forbearance

Realistic Timeline: Recognize that it could take a few weeks or even months to identify trigger foods and see improvements, and that effects might not be seen right away.

Practice Patience: Throughout the elimination period, have patience with yourself or your child. Keep in mind that making dietary adjustments can be difficult but also beneficial.

To sum up, getting ready for an elimination diet for ADHD entails a mix of realistic goal-setting, professional advice, and self-evaluation. Through comprehensive evaluation of ADHD symptoms, identification of possible triggers, symptom monitoring, and consultation with medical professionals, people can start their elimination diet with a well-informed and organized strategy, improving the chances of successful ADHD symptom management.

Chapter 3

Commencing the Diet of Elimination

An elimination diet's initial phase is an important stage in the procedure. In order to determine which foods may be aggravating your symptoms of ADHD, it entails temporarily eliminating possible trigger foods from your diet. The following are the necessary components to begin the elimination diet:

Phase of Elimination

The main component of the diet is the elimination phase, which can last anywhere from a few weeks to many months, depending on personal needs and objectives. You will cut out particular foods or dietary groups that you believe could be generating negative reactions during this time. This phase consists of the following two main parts:

Determine Trigger things: Make a thorough list of all the things you should cut out of your diet based on your previous evaluation of possible trigger foods. This list should include foods like artificial additives, high-sugar snacks, and gluten-containing products that are known to affect symptoms of ADHD.

Make a Meal Plan: Create a menu that emphasizes complete, unadulterated foods. Include foods that don't include any of the recognized triggers to make sure your nutritional demands are satisfied. A range of fruits, vegetables, lean meats, and gluten-free grains should be included.

Meal Preparation: To make following your elimination diet easier, think about bulk cooking and meal preparation. Making meals that are easy to eliminate will help you avoid giving in to the lure of trigger foods.

Purchasing Foods That Ensure Elimination

Make a Shopping List: Create a thorough shopping list that supports your elimination strategy before you go to the grocery store. Make sure it has everything you need to prepare your meals that are elimination-friendly.

Read Labels Carefully: Carefully check ingredient labels when purchasing packaged foods to steer clear of products that include artificial additives, preservatives, or other possible triggers. Additionally, keep an eye out for any unreported sugar sources.

Investigate Specialty Sections: A lot of supermarkets include sections specifically for gluten-free or allergy-free goods. Look through these sections to identify acceptable replacements for the foods you typically eat.

Fresh Produce: Since fresh produce is usually devoid of artificial additives and preservatives, it is best to buy it that way. To make sure your diet is well-balanced, choose a range of vibrant produce.

Lean Proteins: Opt for lean protein sources including fish, lentils, and skinless chicken. Processed meats should be avoided since they could have additives.

Alternative Grains: If you're cutting out gluten, consider gluten-free varieties of rice, quinoa, and oats. These can be used as wholesome alternatives to products made with wheat.

You must be consistent and follow the plan to the letter when you start the elimination diet. To keep track of your meals and any changes in your symptoms of ADHD, keep a food journal. When it comes time to reintroduce foods during the following phase of the diet, this record will be helpful. To make sure that your food choices stay nutritionally sufficient and balanced throughout the process, get advice and support from a certified dietitian or healthcare professional.

Chapter 4

Recognizing Allergens and Trigger Foods

One of the most important steps in using an elimination diet to manage ADHD symptoms is figuring out what foods and allergies to avoid. Through awareness of the foods that might worsen symptoms, people can adjust their diet to support improved concentration, focus, and mood. The next section will address the essential components involved in determining trigger foods and allergens:

Common Culprits

There's a popular belief that eating certain foods makes symptoms of ADHD worse. ***They consist of:***

Food Dye and Artificial Additives: Several research have looked into the possible connection between food dyes (like Red 40) and artificial additives (like food coloring), particularly in child populations. Often, processed snacks, sugary cereals, and candies with vibrant colors contain these chemicals.

rich in added sugars and refined carbohydrates: Consuming foods high in these nutrients can cause blood sugar levels to rise and fall, which may have an impact on mood and attentiveness. Among them are soft drinks, candy, and sugary munchies.

Preservatives and Artificial Additives

Artificial preservatives and additives can be included in processed foods and can go by different names on ingredient lists. Though it can be difficult, it's crucial to recognize and stay away from these. *Typical preservatives and additions are as follows:*

Food dyes: These are synthetic colorings, such as Red 40, Yellow 5, and Blue 1, that are frequently used in processed foods, sweets, and beverages.

Preservatives BHA and BHT: These are added to snacks and processed meats, among other things, to increase their shelf life.

Monosodium glutamate, or MSG: is an ingredient in various processed and savory meals. While it's known to improve flavor, some people may react negatively to it.

Allergens and Sensitivities to Food

Each person has a different set of allergies and food sensitivities. It is crucial to identify and take care of these sensitivities, which could include:

Dairy: Some people may be allergic to dairy products or have a lactose intolerance, which can cause digestive problems and perhaps exacerbate symptoms of ADHD.

Nuts: It's important to treat nut allergies carefully since they can have serious consequences, especially if they affect peanuts and tree nuts.

Sugar's and Refined Carbohydrates' Part

Determining the dietary triggers for symptoms of ADHD requires an understanding of the role of refined carbs and sugar. This comprises:

A. The Effect of Sugar on ADHD

Blood Sugar Fluctuations: Sugar- and refined carbohydrate-rich foods can quickly raise and then drop blood sugar levels. These variations could be a factor in mood swings and difficulty focusing.

Dopamine Release: Sugar has the ability to momentarily raise dopamine levels, which are linked to pleasure and reward. This can provide a brief period of attention and motivation in ADHD sufferers, which is followed by a "crash."

Processed meals: You may be surprised to learn that sugar is frequently added to processed meals like bread, sauces, and salad dressings.

Low-Fat items: Occasionally, sugars are added to low-fat items to improve flavor.

The Relationship Between Gluten

The protein gluten, which is present in wheat, barley, and rye, has drawn attention in relation to managing ADHD:

A. ADHD and gluten

Sensitivity: Some people may be sensitive to gluten, which can lead to mood swings, mental fog, and intestinal pain.

Celiac Disease: People with celiac disease, an autoimmune disorder brought on by gluten, may occasionally have neurological symptoms that resemble ADHD.

Gluten-Free Substitutes: If gluten sensitivity is suspected, you might want to try rice, quinoa, and maize as gluten-free alternatives to grains that contain gluten.

Reading Labels: Because gluten can lurk in unexpected places, such sauces and processed meals, make sure to carefully read food labels to confirm that the product is gluten-free.

It's crucial to remember that while some people with ADHD may find that specific foods and additives trigger them, other people may not be impacted by the same things. It takes close observation, documentation, and, in certain situations, expert advice from a medical professional or certified nutritionist to identify one's own trigger foods. Under the guidance of a professional, an exclusion diet can help identify particular food triggers and result in more successful treatment of ADHD symptoms.

Shopping friendly list with tips

Shopping for ADHD-friendly foods and maintaining a balanced diet is crucial for managing ADHD symptoms effectively. *Below is a list of shopping items along with tips for selecting and incorporating them into your diet:*

Fruits:

Items: Apples, bananas, berries (strawberries, blueberries, raspberries), oranges, grapes, watermelon, kiwi, and other fresh fruits.

Tips: Opt for a variety of fruits rich in fiber and vitamins. Buy in-season fruits for better flavor and affordability.

Vegetables:

Items: Leafy greens, broccoli, carrots, bell peppers, cucumbers, sweet potatoes, and any vegetables you enjoy.

Tips: Choose a rainbow of colors for a range of nutrients. Fresh and frozen options are both nutritious.

Whole Grains:

Items: Oats, brown rice, quinoa, whole wheat pasta, whole grain bread, and whole grain cereal.

Tips: Look for whole grains with minimal processing and high fiber content. Avoid products with added sugars.

Lean Proteins:

Items: Skinless poultry, lean cuts of beef, fish (especially fatty fish like salmon), tofu, and legumes.

Tips: Go for lean proteins, and try to include fatty fish for omega-3 fatty acids, which can benefit ADHD.

Dairy or Dairy Alternatives:

Items: Low-fat dairy, almond milk, soy milk, or other non-dairy options.

Tips: Choose unsweetened dairy alternatives to reduce added sugars. Dairy products may be an excellent source of vitamin D and calcium.

Nuts and Seeds:

Items: Almonds, walnuts, chia seeds, flaxseeds, and pumpkin seeds.

Tips: These are excellent sources of healthy fats and protein. Use them as snacks or to add texture to dishes.

Healthy Fats:

Items: Avocado, olive oil, and fatty fish like salmon or mackerel.

Tips: Incorporate these healthy fats into your cooking for improved brain health and focus.

Fresh Herbs and Spices:

Items: Basil, thyme, oregano, cinnamon, turmeric, and others for flavor and nutrition.

Tips: Herbs and spices can enhance the taste of your dishes without added salt or sugar.

Sweeteners:

Items: Honey, maple syrup, or stevia for occasional sweetening needs.

Tips: Use these natural sweeteners sparingly when needed to reduce sugar intake.

Hydration:

Items: Water, herbal teas, and 100% fruit juices in moderation.

Tips: Staying hydrated is vital for focus. Opt for water as the primary beverage.

Snack Options:

Items: Rice cakes, nut butter, fresh fruit, vegetables, and hummus.

Tips: Choose nutrient-dense snacks to maintain steady energy levels throughout the day.

Canned or Frozen Foods:

Items: Canned salmon, frozen fruits and vegetables, and low-sodium canned soups.

Tips: Keep these as convenient options for when you're short on time.

Dark Chocolate:

Items: Dark chocolate (70% cocoa or higher) for occasional sweet cravings.

Tips: Dark chocolate can be a healthier treat in moderation.

Supplements:

Items: Omega-3 fatty acid supplements (e.g., fish oil) and multivitamins.

Tips: Consult with a healthcare professional before taking supplements to address specific nutrient needs.

Non-Food Items:

Items: Airtight containers for storing foods, a food scale for portion control, and a shopping list to stay organized.

Tips: Keeping food fresh and properly portioned can help maintain a balanced diet.

Create a meal plan and gather ADHD-friendly recipes to help guide your shopping and meal preparation.

Schedule a consultation with a registered dietitian to receive personalized guidance on your ADHD-friendly diet.

Remember, while shopping for ADHD-friendly foods is important, maintaining a balanced diet is a long-term commitment. Planning your meals, staying hydrated, and consulting with healthcare professionals are all key elements of successfully managing ADHD through diet. Choose a variety of nutrient-rich foods, practice portion control, and enjoy the journey towards improved focus and well-being.

Knowing which foods to include (safe and nutrient-rich options) and which to avoid (possible trigger foods) is crucial when starting an elimination diet for ADHD control. Remember that each person has different dietary triggers, therefore customization is essential. As a general rule of thumb:

Items to Steer Clear of (Foods That May Trigger):

Avoid foods and beverages that include artificial flavors, preservatives, and colors (such as Red 40 and Yellow 5). *These are frequently present in sugary cereals, processed snacks, and some drinks.*

High Sugar and Sugary Snacks: Restrict or avoid foods that have a lot of added sugar, such as sweetened beverages, candy, sugary cereals, and pastries. Be mindful of any hidden sugars in sauces and condiments.

Reduce your intake of highly processed and quick food items, as they frequently include artificial additives, harmful trans fats, and excessive sodium.

Gluten and Wheat Products: Steer clear of wheat-based foods like bread, pasta, and pastries if you have a suspected gluten sensitivity. Choose gluten-free substitutes such as maize, quinoa, and rice.

Dairy Products: Milk, cheese, and yogurt are examples of dairy products that people with suspected lactose intolerances or sensitivities should avoid. Try looking for dairy-free substitutes such as coconut yogurt or almond milk.

Soy Products: For certain people, soy may cause allergies. Steer clear of anything that contains soy, such as edamame, tofu, and soy milk.

Common Allergenic Nuts: Steer clear of peanuts and tree nuts like almonds, cashews, and walnuts if there is a history of nut allergies.

Processed Meats: Avoid processed meats because they could have preservatives and additives. Examples of these are hot dogs, sausages, and bacon.

Foods to Add (Safe and Nutrient-Rich Selections):

Fresh Fruits and veggies: Include a range of vibrant fruits and veggies in your diet because they are a great source of antioxidants, vitamins, and minerals. Berries, leafy greens, citrus fruits, and other foods can be among them.

Lean Proteins: Choose lean protein sources such as fish, poultry, lentils, chickpeas, and black beans. Salmon and other fish high in omega-3 fatty acids are very good for the brain.

Whole Grains: If you're trying to avoid gluten, go for whole grains like brown rice, quinoa, and oats as well as gluten-free grains like amaranth or teff.

Healthy Fats: Include foods high in healthy fats, such as avocados, olive oil, nuts (if they aren't allergic), and seeds (such as chia or flaxseeds). Walnuts, flaxseeds, and fatty fish are good sources of omega-3 fatty acids, which can be particularly helpful.

Dairy substitutes: If you're trying to stay away from dairy, consider dairy substitutes like almond milk, coconut yogurt, or vegan cheese made without soy.

Water: Make water your main beverage to be well hydrated. Steer clear of excessive caffeine and sugary drinks.

Meals Made at Home: Cooking at home gives you more control over the ingredients and caliber of the food you eat.

Nutrient Supplements: See a doctor or nutritionist if you have concerns about nutrient deficiencies to find out if you need to take multivitamins or omega-3 supplements.

Keep in mind that precise identification of trigger foods and strict adherence to the meal plan are essential for the success of an elimination diet. It's best to collaborate with a medical professional or qualified dietitian who can offer advice, track developments, and guarantee that dietary requirements are satisfied all along the way. Be patient and give the diet some time to demonstrate its potential benefits in treating symptoms of ADHD, as individual responses to dietary modifications differ.

Chapter 5

Meal planning

Day 1:

Breakfast: Tofu Scramble

Lunch: Quinoa Salad with Chickpeas and Veggies

Dinner: Baked Salmon with Lemon and Dill

Day 2:

Breakfast: Oatmeal with Berries

Lunch: Turkey and Avocado Wrap

Dinner: Stir-Fried Tofu with Vegetables

Breakfast: Greek Yogurt Parfait with Honey and Nuts

Lunch: Hummus and Veggie Sandwich

Dinner: Brown Rice and Black Bean Casserole

Breakfast: Scrambled Eggs with Spinach

Lunch: Lentil Soup

Dinner: Baked Chicken with Roasted Vegetables

Breakfast: Peanut Butter and Banana Smoothie

Lunch: Grilled Chicken Salad

Dinner: Spinach and Mushroom Stuffed Chicken

Breakfast: Whole-Grain Pancakes with Blueberries

Lunch: Sushi Rolls with Brown Rice

Dinner: Beef and Broccoli Stir-Fry

Breakfast: Chia Seed Pudding with Fresh Fruit

Lunch: Sweet Potato and Black Bean Burrito

Dinner: Spaghetti with Tomato and Basil Sauce

Breakfast: Vegetable Omelette

Lunch: Greek Salad with Feta and Olives

Dinner: Veggie Stir-Fry with Quinoa

Breakfast: Overnight Oats with Almonds and Chia Seeds

Lunch: Tuna Salad with Spinach

Dinner: Teriyaki Salmon with Asparagus

Breakfast: Smoked Salmon Bagel with Cream Cheese

Lunch: Baked Potato with Broccoli and Cheese

Dinner: Pork Tenderloin with Sweet Potatoes

Day 11:

Breakfast: Sliced Apples with Almond Butter

Lunch: Roasted Brussels Sprouts

Dinner: Quinoa Salad with Chickpeas and Veggies

Day 12:

Breakfast: Carrot Sticks with Hummus

Lunch: Garlic Mashed Cauliflower

Dinner: Baked Salmon with Lemon and Dill

Day 13:

Breakfast: Greek Yogurt with Berries

Lunch: Baked Sweet Potato Fries

Dinner: Peanut Butter and Banana Smoothie

Day 14:

Breakfast: Trail Mix with Nuts and Dried Fruit

Lunch: Brown Rice with Sautéed Mushrooms

Dinner: Tofu Scramble

Day 15:

Breakfast: Cottage Cheese with Pineapple

Lunch: Cucumber and Tomato Salad

Dinner: Beef and Broccoli Stir-Fry

Day 16:

Breakfast: Guacamole with Whole-Grain Crackers

Lunch: Butternut Squash Soup

Dinner: Spinach and Mushroom Stuffed Chicken

Day 17:

Breakfast: Rice Cakes with Avocado

Lunch: Creamy Coleslaw with Greek Yogurt Dressing

Dinner: Baked Chicken with Roasted Vegetables

Breakfast: Celery Sticks with Peanut Butter

Lunch: Beet and Walnut Salad

Dinner: Veggie Stir-Fry with Quinoa

Breakfast: Popcorn with Herbs and Olive Oil

Lunch: Lentil Soup

Dinner: Teriyaki Salmon with Asparagus

Breakfast: Sliced Cucumber with Tzatziki

Lunch: Sushi Rolls with Brown Rice

Dinner: Pork Tenderloin with Sweet Potatoes

Breakfast: Fruity Yogurt Popsicles

Lunch: Hummus and Veggie Sandwich

Dinner: Spaghetti with Tomato and Basil Sauce

ADHD elimination diet Breakfast recipe

Tofu Scramble:

Ingredients:

1/2 block of firm tofu, crumbled

1/2 cup diced bell peppers

1/2 cup diced onions

1/2 cup chopped spinach

1/2 teaspoon turmeric

Salt and pepper to taste

Olive oil for cooking

Preparation:

In a pan set over medium heat, warm the olive oil.

Add diced bell peppers and onions. Sauté until they soften.

Add crumbled tofu, turmeric, and chopped spinach.

Cook until the tofu resembles scrambled eggs.

Season with salt and pepper.

Instructions:

Serve as a breakfast scramble with whole-grain toast and fresh fruit.

Cooking Time: 15 minutes

Serving Size: 1 serving

Nutrition Value (approx. per serving):

Calories: 250

Protein: 15g

Carbohydrates: 10g

Fiber: 3g

Fat: 17g

Oatmeal with Berries:

Ingredients:

1/2 cup rolled oats

1 cup almond milk

1/2 cup mixed berries (e.g., strawberries, blueberries, raspberries)

1 tablespoon honey

1/2 teaspoon cinnamon

Preparation:

Almond milk and rolled oats should be combined in a saucepan.

Cook over medium heat, stirring, until the oatmeal thickens.

Top with mixed berries, honey, and a sprinkle of cinnamon.

Instructions:

Serve as a warm oatmeal breakfast.

Cooking Time: 10 minutes

Serving Size: 1 serving

Nutrition Value (approx. per serving):

Calories: 300

Protein: 6g

Carbohydrates: 55g

Fiber: 9g

Fat: 6g

Greek Yogurt Parfait with Honey and Nuts:

Ingredients:

1 cup Greek yogurt

2 tablespoons honey

2 tablespoons chopped mixed nuts (e.g., almonds, walnuts)

1/2 cup mixed berries

Preparation:

Arrange a mixture of berries on top of Greek yogurt in a glass or bowl.

Drizzle honey on top.

Sprinkle with chopped nuts.

Instructions:

Serve as a yogurt parfait for breakfast.

Cooking Time: 5 minutes (no cooking required)

Serving Size: 1 serving

Nutrition Value (approx. per serving):

Calories: 350

Protein: 20g

Carbohydrates: 30g

Fiber: 3g

Fat: 18g

Scrambled Eggs with Spinach:

Ingredients:

2 eggs

1/2 cup chopped spinach

Salt and pepper to taste

Olive oil for cooking

Preparation:

In a bowl, whisk together eggs and add pepper and salt to taste.

In a pan set over medium heat, warm the olive oil.

Add chopped spinach and sauté until wilted.

Pour the whisked eggs into the pan and scramble until cooked.

Instructions:

Serve as scrambled eggs with whole-grain toast and sliced tomatoes.

Cooking Time: 10 minutes

Serving Size: 1 serving

Nutrition Value (approx. per serving):

Calories: 200

Protein: 15g

Carbohydrates: 2g

Fiber: 1g

Fat: 15g

Peanut Butter and Banana:

Ingredients:

1 ripe banana

2 tablespoons peanut butter

1 cup almond milk

1 teaspoon honey (optional)

Ice cubes (optional)

Preparation:

Blend together the ripe banana, ice cubes, almond milk, peanut butter, and honey using a blender.

Blend until smooth.

Instructions:

Serve as a creamy peanut butter and banana smoothie.

Preparation Time: 5 minutes

Serving Size: 1 serving

Nutrition Value (approx. per serving):

Calories: 350

Protein: 10g

Carbohydrates: 25g

Fiber: 4g

Fat: 20g

Whole-Grain Pancakes with Blueberries:

Ingredients:

1 cup whole-grain pancake mix

1 cup almond milk

1/2 cup fresh blueberries

Olive oil for cooking

Preparation:

In a bowl, combine the whole-grain pancake mix and almond milk until you have a smooth batter.

Gently fold in the fresh blueberries.

In a skillet over medium heat, warm the olive oil.

Pour a ladle of pancake batter onto the skillet.

Cook until surface bubbles appear, then turn and continue cooking until golden brown.

Instructions:

Serve as whole-grain blueberry pancakes with a drizzle of honey.

Cooking Time: 15 minutes

Serving Size: 2 pancakes

Nutrition Value (approx. per serving):

Calories: 300

Protein: 8g

Carbohydrates: 60g

Fiber: 10g

Fat: 5g

Chia Seed Pudding with Fresh Fruit:

Ingredients:

2 tablespoons chia seeds

1 cup almond milk

1/2 cup fresh mixed fruit (e.g., strawberries, kiwi, pineapple)

1/2 teaspoon honey (optional)

Preparation:

Almond milk and chia seeds should be combined in a bowl.

When it starts to thicken, give it a good stir and chill for at least two hours or overnight.

Top with fresh mixed fruit and drizzle with honey if desired.

Instructions:

Serve as chia seed pudding with a variety of fresh fruits.

Preparation Time: 2 hours or overnight (no cooking required)

Serving Size: 1 serving

Nutrition Value (approx. per serving):

Calories: 200

Protein: 4g

Carbohydrates: 30g

Fiber: 10g

Fat: 7g

Ingredients:

2 eggs

1/2 cup diced bell peppers

1/2 cup diced onions

1/2 cup sliced mushrooms

Salt and pepper to taste

Olive oil for cooking

Preparation:

In a bowl, whisk together eggs and add pepper and salt to taste.

In a pan set over medium heat, warm the olive oil.

Add diced bell peppers, onions, and sliced mushrooms. Sauté until they soften.

Pour the whisked eggs into the pan and cook until set.

Instructions:

Serve as a vegetable omelette with a side of whole-grain toast.

Cooking Time: 10 minutes

Serving Size: 1 serving

Nutrition Value (approx. per serving):

Calories: 220

Protein: 12g

Carbohydrates: 10g

Fiber: 3g

Fat: 15g

Overnight Oats with Almonds and Chia Seeds:

Ingredients:

1/2 cup rolled oats

1 cup almond milk

1 tablespoon chia seeds

1/4 cup sliced almonds

1/2 teaspoon vanilla extract

1/2 teaspoon honey (optional)

Preparation:

In a jar or bowl, combine rolled oats, almond milk, chia seeds, sliced almonds, vanilla extract, and honey (if desired).

Mix well, cover, and refrigerate overnight.

Instructions:

Serve as overnight oats with a sprinkle of additional sliced almonds and a drizzle of honey.

Preparation Time: Overnight (no cooking required)

Serving Size: 1 serving

Nutrition Value (approx. per serving):

Calories: 350

Protein: 10g

Carbohydrates: 40g

Fiber: 10g

Fat: 18g

Smoked Salmon Bagel with Cream Cheese:

Ingredients:

1 whole-grain bagel

2 ounces smoked salmon

2 tablespoons cream cheese

1/4 cup sliced cucumber

1/4 cup sliced red onion

1/2 teaspoon capers

Preparation:

Slice the whole-grain bagel in half.

Spread cream cheese on both halves.

Layer smoked salmon, sliced cucumber, red onion, and capers on one half.

Top with the other bagel half.

Instructions:

Serve as a smoked salmon bagel with cream cheese.

Preparation Time: 10 minutes (no cooking required)

Serving Size: 1 serving

Nutrition Value (approx. per serving):

Calories: 350

Protein: 18g

Carbohydrates: 30g

Fiber: 6g

Fat: 15g

Lunch recipes

Grilled Chicken Salad

Ingredients:

2 boneless, skinless chicken breasts

1 tablespoon olive oil

Salt and pepper to taste

Mixed greens (e.g., lettuce, spinach)

Cherry tomatoes

Cucumber slices

Red onion, thinly sliced

Balsamic vinaigrette dressing

Preparation:

Preheat the grill or grill pan.

Add salt and pepper to the chicken breasts after brushing them with olive oil.

Cook the chicken for 6 to 8 minutes on each side, or until it's thoroughly done.

Slice the chicken into strips.

Arrange mixed greens on a plate and top with chicken, cherry tomatoes, cucumber, and red onion.

Drizzle with balsamic vinaigrette dressing.

Instructions:

Serve as a salad.

Cooking Time: 15 minutes

Serving Size: 1 salad

Nutrition Value (approx. per serving):

Calories: 350

Protein: 30g

Carbohydrates: 10g

Fiber: 3g

Fat: 20g

Ingredients:

Nori seaweed sheets

Cooked brown rice

Sliced avocado

Sliced cucumber

Cooked crab or imitation crab (optional)

Soy sauce

Pickled ginger

Wasabi

Preparation:

Place a bamboo sushi rolling mat on a flat surface.

Place a plastic wrap sheet on top of the bamboo mat.

Place a nori sheet over the plastic wrap.

Wet your hands and press a thin layer of brown rice over the nori, leaving about 1 inch of nori uncovered at the top.

Arrange sliced avocado, cucumber, and crab (if using) in the center of the rice.

Roll the bamboo mat, pressing the ingredients into a tight cylinder.

Remove the roll from the mat, and slice it into bite-sized pieces.

Serve with soy sauce, pickled ginger, and wasabi.

Instructions:

Serve as sushi rolls.

Preparation Time: 30 minutes

Serving Size: Varies

Nutrition Value (approx. per serving):

Calories: 200 (varies based on ingredients)

Protein: 5g (varies)

Carbohydrates: 40g (varies)

Fiber: 5g (varies)

Fat: 2g (varies)

Sweet Potato and Black Bean Burrito

Ingredients:

Whole-grain tortilla

Cooked and mashed sweet potatoes

Canned black beans, drained and rinsed

Sliced avocado

Salsa

Chopped cilantro

Lime juice

Salt and pepper

Preparation:

Lay the whole-grain tortilla flat.

Spread mashed sweet potatoes on the tortilla.

Top with black beans, sliced avocado, salsa, cilantro, and a squeeze of lime juice.

Season with salt and pepper.

Roll up the tortilla.

Instructions:

Serve as a burrito.

Cooking Time: 15 minutes

Serving Size: 1 burrito

Nutrition Value (approx. per serving):

Calories: 350

Protein: 10g

Carbohydrates: 60g

Fiber: 12g

Fat: 8g

Ingredients:

Mixed greens (e.g., lettuce, spinach)

Cucumber slices

Cherry tomatoes

Red onion, thinly sliced

Kalamata olives

Crumbled feta cheese

Balsamic vinaigrette dressing

Preparation:

Arrange mixed greens on a plate.

Top with cucumber, cherry tomatoes, red onion, Kalamata olives, and crumbled feta cheese.

Drizzle with balsamic vinaigrette dressing.

Instructions:

Serve as a salad.

Preparation Time: 10 minutes

Serving Size: 1 salad

Nutrition Value (approx. per serving):

Calories: 300

Protein: 8g

Carbohydrates: 15g

Fiber: 5g

Fat: 25g

Tuna Salad with Spinach

Ingredients:

Canned tuna, drained

Greek yogurt or mayonnaise

Diced celery

Diced red onion

Lemon juice

Salt and pepper

Fresh spinach leaves

Preparation:

In a bowl, combine canned tuna, Greek yogurt or mayonnaise, diced celery, diced red onion, and a squeeze of lemon juice.

Season with salt and pepper.

Serve the tuna salad over a bed of fresh spinach leaves.

Instructions:

Serve as a salad.

Preparation Time: 10 minutes

Serving Size: 1 salad

Nutrition Value (approx. per serving):

Calories: 250

Protein: 25g

Carbohydrates: 5g

Fiber: 2g

Fat: 15g

Baked Potato with Broccoli and Cheese

Ingredients:

Russet potato

Broccoli florets

Shredded cheddar cheese

Greek yogurt or sour cream

Chopped chives

Salt and pepper

Preparation:

Preheat the oven to 400°F (200°C).

Wash and dry the russet potato.

Prick the potato with a fork and place it on a baking sheet.

Bake the potato for 45 to 60 minutes, or until it is soft.

Steam or boil broccoli florets until tender.

Cut the baked potato open and fluff the insides with a fork.

Top with steamed broccoli, shredded cheddar cheese, Greek yogurt or sour cream, chopped chives, and season with salt and pepper.

Instructions:

Serve as a baked potato.

Cooking Time: 60 minutes

Serving Size: 1 potato

Nutrition Value (approx. per serving):

Calories: 350

Protein: 10g

Carbohydrates: 45g

Fiber: 5g

Fat: 15g

Quinoa Salad with Chickpeas and Veggies

Ingredients:

1 cup quinoa

2 cups water

1 can chickpeas, drained and rinsed

1 cup diced cucumber

1 cup cherry tomatoes, halved

1/2 cup diced red bell pepper

1/4 cup diced red onion

1/4 cup fresh parsley, chopped

3 tablespoons olive oil

2 tablespoons lemon juice

Salt and pepper to taste

Preparation:

Rinse quinoa under cold water.

In a saucepan, combine quinoa and water. Bring to a boil, then simmer for 15 to 20 minutes while lowering the heat and covering.

Fluff quinoa with a fork and let it cool.

In a large bowl, combine quinoa, chickpeas, cucumber, tomatoes, bell pepper, red onion, and parsley.

In a separate bowl, whisk together olive oil and lemon juice. Season with salt and pepper.

Pour the dressing over the salad and toss to combine.

Instructions:

Serve as a cold salad.

Cooking Time: 20 minutes

Serving Size: 1 1/2 cups

Nutrition Value (approx. per serving):

Calories: 400

Protein: 10g

Carbohydrates: 60g

Fiber: 10g

Fat: 14g

Turkey and Avocado Wrap

Ingredients:

Whole-grain tortilla

Sliced turkey breast

Sliced avocado

Sliced tomato

Lettuce leaves

Greek yogurt or mayonnaise

Mustard

Salt and pepper

Preparation:

Lay the whole-grain tortilla flat.

Spread Greek yogurt or mayonnaise and mustard on the tortilla.

Layer sliced turkey, avocado, tomato, and lettuce on top.

Season with salt and pepper.

Roll up the tortilla tightly.

Instructions:

Serve as a wrap.

Cooking Time: 10 minutes

Serving Size: 1 wrap

Nutrition Value (approx. per serving):

Calories: 350

Protein: 20g

Carbohydrates: 30g

Fiber: 7g

Fat: 18g

Hummus and Veggie Sandwich

Ingredients:

Whole-grain bread

Hummus

Sliced cucumber

Sliced bell peppers

Sliced carrots

Sliced tomato

Sliced red onion

Lettuce leaves

Preparation:

Toast two slices of whole-grain bread and spread with hummus.

Layer cucumber, bell peppers, carrots, tomato, red onion, and lettuce between the slices.

Slice the sandwich in half.

Instructions:

Serve as a sandwich.

Cooking Time: 10 minutes

Serving Size: 1 sandwich

Nutrition Value (approx. per serving):

Calories: 320

Protein: 10g

Carbohydrates: 50g

Fiber: 10g

Fat: 10g

Ingredients:

1 cup dried green or brown lentils

4 cups vegetable broth

1 onion, chopped

2 carrots, chopped

2 celery stalks, chopped

2 cloves garlic, minced

1 teaspoon cumin

1 teaspoon paprika

Salt and pepper to taste

Olive oil for sautéing

Preparation:

Rinse lentils under cold water.

Warm up the olive oil in a big pot over medium heat. Add onions, carrots, and celery, and sauté until tender.

Add minced garlic, cumin, and paprika. Sauté for another minute.

Add lentils and vegetable broth. Bring to a boil, then reduce heat and simmer for 25-30 minutes until lentils are tender.

Season with salt and pepper.

Instructions:

Serve as a hot soup.

Cooking Time: 40 minutes

Serving Size: 2 cups

Nutrition Value (approx. per serving):

Calories: 300

Protein: 18g

Carbohydrates: 55g

Fiber: 18g

Fat: 2g

Dinner recipes

Baked Chicken with Roasted Vegetables:

Ingredients:

4 boneless, skinless chicken breasts

4 cups mixed vegetables (e.g., carrots, bell peppers, zucchini)

2 tablespoons olive oil

1 teaspoon dried rosemary

Salt and pepper to taste

Preparation:

Preheat the oven to 375°F (190°C).

Season chicken breasts with rosemary, salt, and pepper.

Toss vegetables in olive oil, salt, and pepper.

Arrange the vegetables and chicken on a baking sheet..

Instructions:

Bake until the chicken is cooked through, 25 to 30 minutes.

Accompany with quinoa or brown rice on the side.

Cooking Time: 25-30 minutes

Serving Size: 1 chicken breast with vegetables

Nutrition Value (approx. per serving):

Calories: 350

Protein: 40g

Carbohydrates: 15g

Fiber: 5g

Fat: 15g

Ingredients:

4 boneless, skinless chicken breasts

2 cups fresh spinach

1 cup mushrooms (sliced)

1/2 cup low-fat cream cheese

1/4 cup grated Parmesan cheese

2 cloves garlic (minced)

Salt and pepper to taste

Preparation:

Preheat the oven to 375°F (190°C).

Sauté garlic and mushrooms in a pan until they are soft.

Add spinach and cook until wilted.

Remove from heat and mix in cream cheese, Parmesan, salt, and pepper.

Cut a pocket into each chicken breast and stuff with the spinach and mushroom mixture.

Instructions:

The chicken should be cooked through after 25 to 30 minutes in the oven.

Serve with a side of quinoa or whole-wheat pasta.

Cooking Time: 25-30 minutes

Serving Size: 1 stuffed chicken breast

Nutrition Value (approx. per serving):

Calories: 400

Protein: 40g

Carbohydrates: 10g

Fiber: 3g

Fat: 20g

Ingredients:

1 lb (450g) beef, thinly sliced

4 cups broccoli florets

1/4 cup low-sodium soy sauce

2 tablespoons honey or brown sugar

1 clove garlic (minced)

1 teaspoon ginger (grated)

2 tablespoons vegetable oil

Preparation:

In a bowl, mix soy sauce, honey, garlic, and ginger.

Heat oil in a wok or pan.

Stir-fry beef until browned.

Add broccoli and sauce. Stir-fry until broccoli is tender.

Instructions:

Serve with brown rice or quinoa.

Cooking Time: 20 minutes

Serving Size: 1 cup

Nutrition Value (approx. per serving):

Calories: 350

Protein: 25g

Carbohydrates: 20g

Fiber: 4g

Fat: 20g

Spaghetti with Tomato and Basil Sauce:

Ingredients:

8 oz (225g) whole-wheat spaghetti

2 cups tomato sauce (low-sugar)

1/4 cup fresh basil (chopped)

2 cloves garlic (minced)

1 tablespoon olive oil

Salt and pepper to taste

Preparation:

Cook spaghetti according to package instructions.

Garlic is sautéed in hot olive oil in a pan.

Add tomato sauce, basil, salt, and pepper. Simmer for 10 minutes.

Instructions:

Serve sauce over cooked spaghetti.

Cooking Time: 20 minutes

Serving Size: 1 cup spaghetti with sauce

Nutrition Value (approx. per serving):

Calories: 300

Protein: 10g

Carbohydrates: 60g

Fiber: 8g

Fat: 6g

Veggie Stir-Fry with Quinoa:

Ingredients:

1 cup quinoa

2 cups of mixed stir-fried veggies, such as carrots, snap peas, and bell peppers

2 tablespoons low-sodium soy sauce

1 tablespoon sesame oil

1 teaspoon ginger (grated)

2 cloves garlic (minced)

1 tablespoon vegetable oil

Preparation:

Rinse quinoa and cook according to package instructions.

Heat up some vegetable oil in a skillet or wok.

Add the garlic and ginger to the veggies and stir-fry until soft.

Add cooked quinoa, soy sauce, and sesame oil. Stir-fry for 2 minutes.

Instructions:

Serve as a quinoa stir-fry.

Cooking Time: 25 minutes

Serving Size: 1 cup

Nutrition Value (approx. per serving):

Calories: 350

Protein: 10g

Carbohydrates: 60g

Fiber: 7g

Fat: 8g

Ingredients:

4 salmon fillets

1 lb (450g) asparagus

1/4 cup low-sodium teriyaki sauce

2 tablespoons honey or brown sugar

1 clove garlic (minced)

1 teaspoon ginger (grated)

2 tablespoons vegetable oil

Preparation:

In a bowl, mix teriyaki sauce, honey, garlic, and ginger.

In a pan, heat vegetable oil.

Sear salmon fillets until golden brown.

Add asparagus and sauce. Cook until asparagus is tender.

Instructions:

Accompany with quinoa or brown rice on the side.

Cooking Time: 20 minutes

Serving Size: 1 salmon fillet with asparagus

Nutrition Value (approx. per serving):

Calories: 380

Protein: 30g

Carbohydrates: 20g

Fiber: 4g

Fat: 20g

Pork Tenderloin with Sweet Potatoes:

Ingredients:

1 pork tenderloin (about 1 lb)

2 large sweet potatoes (cubed)

2 tablespoons olive oil

1 teaspoon dried thyme

1/2 teaspoon paprika

Salt and pepper to taste

Preparation:

Preheat the oven to 375°F (190°C).

In a bowl, toss sweet potato cubes with olive oil, thyme, paprika, salt, and pepper.

Place the pork tenderloin and sweet potatoes on a baking sheet.

Instructions:

Roast for 25-30 minutes until pork is cooked through and sweet potatoes are tender.

After slicing, serve the pork with the sweet potatoes.

Cooking Time: 25-30 minutes

Serving Size: 4 oz pork with sweet potatoes

Nutrition Value (approx. per serving):

Calories: 350

Protein: 30g

Carbohydrates: 25g

Fiber: 4g

Fat: 15g

Baked Salmon with Lemon and Dill:

Ingredients:

4 salmon fillets

2 tablespoons olive oil

2 tablespoons lemon juice

1 tablespoon fresh dill (chopped)

Salt and pepper to taste

Lemon slices for garnish

Preparation:

Preheat the oven to 375°F (190°C).

Place salmon fillets on a baking sheet.

Pour lemon juice and olive oil onto the salmon.

Sprinkle with dill, salt, and pepper.

Arrange slices of lemon over the fillets.

Instructions:

Bake for 15-20 minutes until the salmon is cooked through.

Accompany with a salad or a dish of steaming veggies.

Cooking Time: 15-20 minutes

Serving Size: 1 salmon fillet

Nutrition Value (approx. per serving):

Calories: 350

Protein: 30g

Carbohydrates: 2g

Fiber: 1g

Fat: 24g

Stir-Fried Tofu with Vegetables:

Ingredients:

14 oz (400g) extra-firm tofu, cubed

2 cups mixed stir-fry vegetables (e.g., broccoli, bell peppers, carrots)

2 tablespoons soy sauce

1 tablespoon sesame oil

1 tablespoon honey or maple syrup

1 clove garlic (minced)

1 teaspoon ginger (grated)

1 tablespoon vegetable oil

Preparation:

Cut tofu into cubes after pressing to remove excess water.

In a bowl, mix soy sauce, sesame oil, honey, garlic, and ginger.

In a pan or wok, heat the vegetable oil.

Add tofu and stir-fry until golden brown.

Add vegetables and sauce. Stir-fry until vegetables are tender.

Instructions:

Serve over brown rice or quinoa.

Cooking Time: 20 minutes

Serving Size: 1 cup

Nutrition Value (approx. per serving):

Calories: 320

Protein: 20g

Carbohydrates: 35g

Fiber: 5g

Fat: 12g

Brown Rice and Black Bean Casserole:

Ingredients:

2 cups cooked brown rice

One can (15 oz) of rinsed and drained black beans

1 cup salsa

1 cup shredded cheddar cheese

1 teaspoon cumin

1/2 teaspoon chili powder

1/2 teaspoon garlic powder

Salt and pepper to taste

Preparation:

Preheat the oven to 350°F (175°C).

In a baking dish, mix rice, black beans, salsa, and half of the cheese.

Sprinkle with spices, salt, and pepper.

Top with the remaining cheese.

Instructions:

Bake for 20-25 minutes until the cheese is bubbly.

Serve with steamed veggies or a side salad.

Cooking Time: 20-25 minutes

Serving Size: 1 cup

Nutrition Value (approx. per serving):

Calories: 400

Protein: 15g

Carbohydrates: 50g

Fiber: 9g

Fat: 16g

Sliced Apples with Almond Butter:

Ingredients:

Sliced apples

Almond butter

Preparation:

Wash and slice the apples.

Serve with almond butter for dipping.

Instructions:

Enjoy the sliced apples with a light spread of almond butter.

Cooking Time: No cooking required

Serving Size: 1 serving

Nutrition Value (approx. per serving):

Calories: 150

Protein: 4g

Carbohydrates: 20g

Fiber: 5g

Fat: 7g

Carrot Sticks with Hummus:

Ingredients:

Carrot sticks

Hummus

Preparation:

Wash, peel, and cut the carrots into sticks.

Serve with hummus for dipping.

Instructions:

Dip the carrot sticks into the hummus for a satisfying snack.

Cooking Time: No cooking required

Serving Size: 1 serving

Nutrition Value (approx. per serving):

Calories: 120

Protein: 3g

Carbohydrates: 15g

Fiber: 5g

Fat: 6g

Greek Yogurt with Berries:

Ingredients:

Greek yogurt

Fresh berries (e.g., strawberries, blueberries)

Preparation:

Wash and prepare the berries.

Serve the Greek yogurt in a bowl and top with the berries.

Instructions:

Mix the Greek yogurt and berries for a creamy and nutritious snack.

Cooking Time: No cooking required

Serving Size: 1 serving

Nutrition Value (approx. per serving):

Calories: 180

Protein: 15g

Carbohydrates: 25g

Fiber: 5g

Fat: 3g

Nut-and-fruit-dried trail mix

Ingredients:

Mixed nuts (e.g., almonds, walnuts)

Dried fruits (e.g., raisins, apricots)

Optional: dark chocolate chips

Preparation:

Combine mixed nuts and dried fruits in a bowl.

Optionally, add a small amount of dark chocolate chips.

Instructions:

Enjoy a handful of this trail mix as a crunchy, energy-boosting snack.

Cooking Time: No cooking required

Serving Size: 1 serving

Nutrition Value (approx. per serving):

Calories: 200

Protein: 6g

Carbohydrates: 20g

Fiber: 4g

Fat: 12g

Cottage Cheese with Pineapple:

Ingredients:

Cottage cheese

Fresh pineapple chunks

Preparation:

Prepare fresh pineapple chunks.

Serve cottage cheese in a bowl and top with pineapple.

Instructions:

Mix the cottage cheese and pineapple for a sweet and creamy snack.

Cooking Time: No cooking required

Serving Size: 1 serving

Nutrition Value (approx. per serving):

Calories: 150

Protein: 12g

Carbohydrates: 15g

Fiber: 2g

Fat: 5g

Guacamole with Whole-Grain Crackers:

Ingredients:

Guacamole (avocado, lime, tomato, onion, cilantro)

Whole-grain crackers

Preparation:

Prepare guacamole by mashing avocado and mixing it with lime, tomato, onion, and cilantro.

Serve with whole-grain crackers for dipping.

Instructions:

Dip the whole-grain crackers in the guacamole for a creamy and satisfying snack.

Cooking Time: No cooking required

Serving Size: 1 serving

Nutrition Value (approx. per serving):

Calories: 180

Protein: 3g

Carbohydrates: 15g

Fiber: 5g

Fat: 11g

Rice Cakes with Avocado:

Ingredients:

Rice cakes

Avocado

Preparation:

Slice or mashing the avocado is one option.

Serve the avocado on rice cakes.

Instructions:

Spread the avocado on the rice cakes for a crunchy and creamy snack.

Cooking Time: No cooking required

Serving Size: 1 serving

Nutrition Value (approx. per serving):

Calories: 150

Protein: 2g

Carbohydrates: 20g

Fiber: 4g

Fat: 7g

Celery Sticks with Peanut Butter:

Ingredients:

Celery sticks

Peanut butter

Preparation:

Wash and cut the celery into sticks.

Serve with peanut butter for dipping.

Instructions:

Dip the celery sticks into the peanut butter for a crunchy and nutty snack.

Cooking Time: No cooking required

Serving Size: 1 serving

Nutrition Value (approx. per serving):

Calories: 170

Protein: 4g

Carbohydrates: 8g

Fiber: 4g

Fat: 14g

Popcorn with Herbs and Olive Oil:

Ingredients:

Popcorn kernels

Olive oil

Dried herbs (e.g., rosemary, thyme)

Preparation:

Air-pop the popcorn kernels.

Sprinkle dried herbs over top and drizzle with olive oil.

Instructions:

Enjoy the herbed popcorn for a crunchy and savory snack.

Cooking Time: Varies (depending on your popcorn popper)

Serving Size: 1 serving

Nutrition Value (approx. per serving):

Calories: 100

Protein: 2g

Carbohydrates: 15g

Fiber: 3g

Fat: 4g

Sliced Cucumber with Tzatziki:

Ingredients:

Sliced cucumbers

Tzatziki sauce (yogurt, cucumber, garlic, dill)

Preparation:

Wash and slice the cucumbers.

Serve with tzatziki sauce for dipping.

Instructions:

Dip the cucumber slices into the tzatziki for a refreshing and creamy snack.

Cooking Time: No cooking required

Serving Size: 1 serving

Nutrition Value (approx. per serving):

Calories: 90

Protein: 3g

Carbohydrates: 8g

Fiber: 2g

Fat: 6g

Nutritious Smoothies recipes

Berry Blast Smoothie (with mixed berries)

Ingredients:

1 cup mixed berries (strawberries, blueberries, raspberries)

1/2 cup Greek yogurt

1/2 cup unsweetened almond milk

1 tablespoon honey

Ice cubes (optional)

Preparation:

Wash the berries and prepare your other ingredients.

Instructions:

Combine mixed berries, Greek yogurt, almond milk, honey, and ice cubes (if desired) in a blender.

Blend until smooth.

Serve immediately.

Serving Size: 1 smoothie

Nutrition Value (approx. per serving):

Calories: 200

Protein: 10g

Carbohydrates: 30g

Fiber: 6g

Fat: 5g

Tropical Paradise Smoothie (with mango and pineapple)

Ingredients:

1 cup frozen mango chunks

1/2 cup frozen pineapple chunks

1/2 banana

1/2 cup coconut milk

1/2 cup orange juice

Preparation:

Prepare the frozen fruit, banana, and liquids.

Instructions:

Combine mango, pineapple, banana, coconut milk, and orange juice in a blender.

Blend until smooth.

Serve immediately.

Serving Size: 1 smoothie

Nutrition Value (approx. per serving):

Calories: 250

Protein: 2g

Carbohydrates: 50g

Fiber: 5g

Fat: 6g

Green Machine Smoothie (with spinach and banana)

Ingredients:

1 cup fresh spinach

1 banana

1/2 cup Greek yogurt

1/2 cup unsweetened almond milk

1 tablespoon honey

Preparation:

Wash the spinach, peel the banana, and gather the other ingredients.

Instructions:

Combine fresh spinach, banana, Greek yogurt, almond milk, and honey in a blender.

Blend until smooth.

Serve immediately.

Serving Size: 1 smoothie

Nutrition Value (approx. per serving):

Calories: 200

Protein: 10g

Carbohydrates: 35g

Fiber: 5g

Fat: 3g

Peanut Butter Protein Smoothie

Ingredients:

2 tablespoons natural peanut butter

1 banana

1/2 cup Greek yogurt

1 cup unsweetened almond milk

1 tablespoon honey

Ice cubes (optional)

Preparation:

Gather the peanut butter, banana, Greek yogurt, almond milk, honey, and ice cubes.

Instructions:

Combine peanut butter, banana, Greek yogurt, almond milk, honey, and ice cubes (if desired) in a blender.

Blend until smooth.

Serve immediately.

Serving Size: 1 smoothie

Nutrition Value (approx. per serving):

Calories: 350

Protein: 20g

Carbohydrates: 30g

Fiber: 5g

Fat: 18g

Chocolate Avocado Smoothie

Ingredients:

1/2 ripe avocado

2 tablespoons cocoa powder

1 banana

1 cup almond milk

1 tablespoon honey

Ice cubes (optional)

Preparation:

Cut the avocado and gather the other ingredients.

Instructions:

Combine ripe avocado, cocoa powder, banana, almond milk, honey, and ice cubes (if desired) in a blender.

Blend until smooth.

Serve immediately.

Serving Size: 1 smoothie

Nutrition Value (approx. per serving):

Calories: 280

Protein: 6g

Carbohydrates: 40g

Fiber: 10g

Fat: 12g

Pineapple Coconut Smoothie

Ingredients:

1 cup frozen pineapple chunks

1/2 cup coconut milk

1/2 cup Greek yogurt

1 tablespoon honey

Ice cubes (optional)

Preparation:

Prepare the frozen pineapple, coconut milk, Greek yogurt, honey, and ice cubes.

Instructions:

Combine frozen pineapple, coconut milk, Greek yogurt, honey, and ice cubes (if desired) in a blender.

Blend until smooth.

Serve immediately.

Serving Size: 1 smoothie

Nutrition Value (approx. per serving):

Calories: 220

Protein: 6g

Carbohydrates: 30g

Fiber: 3g

Fat: 10g

Almond Joy Smoothie (with almonds and coconut)

Ingredients:

2 tablespoons shredded coconut

2 tablespoons slivered almonds

1 banana

1 cup almond milk

1 tablespoon honey

Ice cubes (optional)

Preparation:

Gather shredded coconut, slivered almonds, banana, almond milk, honey, and ice cubes.

Instructions:

Combine shredded coconut, slivered almonds, banana, almond milk, honey, and ice cubes (if desired) in a blender.

Blend until smooth.

Serve immediately.

Serving Size: 1 smoothie

Nutrition Value (approx. per serving):

Calories: 280

Protein: 6g

Carbohydrates: 40g

Fiber: 7g

Fat: 12g

Blueberry Bliss Smoothie

Ingredients:

1 cup blueberries (fresh or frozen)

1/2 cup Greek yogurt

1/2 cup unsweetened almond milk

1 tablespoon honey

Ice cubes (optional)

Preparation:

Wash the blueberries and gather the other ingredients.

Instructions:

Combine blueberries, Greek yogurt, almond milk, honey, and ice cubes (if desired) in a blender.

Blend until smooth.

Serve immediately.

Serving Size: 1 smoothie

Nutrition Value (approx. per serving):

Calories: 180

Protein: 10g

Carbohydrates: 30g

Fiber: 5g

Fat: 4g

Ingredients:

1 cup fresh spinach

1 cup kale

1/2 banana

1/2 cup Greek yogurt

1/2 cup unsweetened almond milk

1 tablespoon honey

Preparation:

Wash the spinach and kale, peel the banana, and gather the other ingredients.

Instructions:

Combine fresh spinach, kale, banana, Greek yogurt, almond milk, and honey in a blender.

Blend until smooth.

Serve immediately.

Serving Size: 1 smoothie

Nutrition Value (approx. per serving):

Calories: 200

Protein: 10g

Carbohydrates: 35g

Fiber: 5g

Fat: 3g

Mocha Java Smoothie (with coffee and chocolate)

Ingredients:

1 cup brewed coffee, cooled

1 banana

2 tablespoons cocoa powder

1/2 cup Greek yogurt

1/2 cup almond milk

1 tablespoon honey

Ice cubes (optional)

Preparation:

Brew the coffee and gather the other ingredients.

Instructions:

Combine brewed coffee, banana, cocoa powder, Greek yogurt, almond milk, honey, and ice cubes (if desired) in a blender.

Blend until smooth.

Serve immediately.

Serving Size: 1 smoothie

Nutrition Value (approx. per serving):

Calories: 180

Protein: 10g

Carbohydrates: 30g

Fiber: 5g

Fat: 5g

Dessert recipes

Greek Yogurt and Honey Parfait:

Ingredients:

Greek yogurt

Honey

Mixed berries (e.g., strawberries, blueberries, raspberries)

Granola

Preparation:

In a glass or bowl, layer Greek yogurt, a drizzle of honey, mixed berries, and granola.

Instructions:

Serve chilled.

Serving Size: 1 parfait

Nutrition Value (approx. per serving):

Calories: 300

Protein: 15g

Carbohydrates: 40g

Fiber: 6g

Fat: 10g

Baked Apple with Cinnamon:

Ingredients:

Apples

Cinnamon

Honey (optional)

Preparation:

Preheat the oven to 375°F (190°C).

Core the apples and sprinkle with cinnamon.

Optionally, drizzle with honey.

Place in a baking dish and bake for 25-30 minutes or until tender.

Instructions:

Serve warm.

Cooking Time: 30 minutes

Serving Size: 1 apple

Nutrition Value (approx. per serving):

Calories: 100

Protein: 0g

Carbohydrates: 25g

Fiber: 4g

Fat: 0g

Dark Chocolate Bark with Nuts and Dried Fruit:

Ingredients:

Dark chocolate (70% cocoa or higher)

Mixed nuts (e.g., almonds, walnuts)

Dried fruit (e.g., apricots, cranberries)

Preparation:

Melt dark chocolate in a double boiler or in the microwave.

Stir in mixed nuts and dried fruit.

Transfer the mixture onto a parchment paper-lined baking sheet.

Allow it to cool and harden.

Instructions:

Break into pieces and serve.

Cooking Time: 15 minutes

Serving Size: 1 ounce (approx. one square)

Nutrition Value (approx. per serving):

Calories: 150

Protein: 2g

Carbohydrates: 15g

Fiber: 3g

Fat: 9g

Ingredients:

Almond butter

Rolled oats

Honey

Chia seeds

Dark chocolate chips

Preparation:

In a bowl, mix almond butter, rolled oats, honey, chia seeds, and dark chocolate chips.

Form the mixture into small energy balls.

Instructions:

Chill in the fridge and serve.

Serving Size: 2 energy balls

Nutrition Value (approx. per serving):

Calories: 180

Protein: 5g

Carbohydrates: 15g

Fiber: 3g

Fat: 12g

Coconut Chia Pudding:

Ingredients:

Coconut milk

Chia seeds

Honey (optional)

Vanilla extract

Fresh fruit (e.g., berries)

Preparation:

In a bowl, mix coconut milk, chia seeds, honey, and vanilla extract.

Stir well and refrigerate overnight.

Top with fresh fruit before serving.

Instructions:

Serve chilled.

Serving Size: 1 pudding cup

Nutrition Value (approx. per serving):

Calories: 220

Protein: 5g

Carbohydrates: 15g

Fiber: 7g

Fat: 15g

Mixed Berry Sorbet:

Ingredients:

Mixed berries (e.g., strawberries, blueberries, raspberries)

Lemon juice

Honey (optional)

Preparation:

Blend mixed berries, lemon juice, and honey (if desired) until smooth.

Pour the mixture into an ice cream maker and churn until it reaches a sorbet consistency.

Instructions:

Serve immediately.

Cooking Time: Varies (ice cream maker required)

Serving Size: 1 scoop

Nutrition Value (approx. per serving):

Calories: 80

Protein: 1g

Carbohydrates: 20g

Fiber: 4g

Fat: 0g

Cinnamon Baked Pears:

Ingredients:

Pears

Cinnamon

Honey (optional)

Preparation:

Preheat the oven to 375°F (190°C).

Slice the pears and place them in a baking dish.

Add a dash of cinnamon and, if preferred, some honey.

Bake for 20-25 minutes or until tender.

Instructions:

Serve warm.

Cooking Time: 25 minutes

Serving Size: 1 pear

Nutrition Value (approx. per serving):

Calories: 100

Protein: 1g

Carbohydrates: 25g

Fiber: 6g

Fat: 0g

Avocado Chocolate Mousse:

Ingredients:

Avocados

Cocoa powder

Honey (or maple syrup)

Vanilla extract

Preparation:

In a blender, combine avocados, cocoa powder, honey (or maple syrup), and vanilla extract.

Blend until smooth.

Instructions:

Refrigerate and serve chilled.

Serving Size: 1/2 cup

Nutrition Value (approx. per serving):

Calories: 200

Protein: 3g

Carbohydrates: 20g

Fiber: 8g

Fat: 14g

Banana Walnut Muffins:

Ingredients:

Ripe bananas

Whole wheat flour

Chopped walnuts

Honey (or maple syrup)

Baking powder

Cinnamon

Preparation:

As you prepare a muffin tin, line it with paper liners and preheat the oven to 350°F/175°C.

In a bowl, mash bananas and add whole wheat flour, chopped walnuts, honey (or maple syrup), baking powder, and cinnamon.

Mix well and divide the batter into muffin cups.

Bake for 20-25 minutes or until the muffins are firm and golden.

Instructions:

Serve as muffins.

Cooking Time: 25 minutes

Serving Size: 2 muffins

Nutrition Value (approx. per serving):

Calories: 250

Protein: 5g

Carbohydrates: 40g

Fiber: 5g

Fat: 8g

Fruity Yogurt Popsicles:

Ingredients:

Greek yogurt

Mixed berries (e.g., strawberries, blueberries, raspberries)

Honey

Preparation:

Blend together Greek yogurt, mixed berries, and honey using a blender.

Blend until smooth.

Fill popsicle molds with ingredients, then insert sticks.

Freeze until solid.

Instructions:

Serve as popsicles.

Cooking Time: Varies (freezing time)

Serving Size: 1 popsicle

Nutrition Value (approx. per serving):

Calories: 70

Protein: 4g

Carbohydrates: 12g

Fiber: 2g

Fat: 1g

Roasted Brussels Sprouts

Ingredients:

Brussels sprouts

Olive oil

Salt and pepper

Optional: garlic powder, grated Parmesan cheese

Preparation:

Preheat the oven to 400°F (200°C).

Trim and halve Brussels sprouts.

Toss with olive oil, salt, pepper, and any optional

seasonings.

Spread on a baking sheet.

Instructions:

Roast in the oven for 25-30 minutes until they're tender and browned.

Cooking Time: 25-30 minutes

Serving Size: 1 cup

Nutrition Value (approx. per serving):

Calories: 70

Protein: 3g

Carbohydrates: 9g

Fiber: 3g

Fat: 3g

Ingredients:

Cauliflower

Garlic cloves

Olive oil

Salt and pepper

Greek yogurt

Preparation:

Steam or boil cauliflower until tender.

Sauté garlic in olive oil until fragrant.

Combine cooked cauliflower, sautéed garlic, olive oil, Greek yogurt, salt, and pepper in a food processor.

Instructions:

Blend until smooth.

Cooking Time: 20 minutes

Serving Size: 1 cup

Nutrition Value (approx. per serving):

Calories: 70

Protein: 4g

Carbohydrates: 10g

Fiber: 5g

Fat: 2g

Quinoa Pilaf with Vegetables

Ingredients:

Quinoa

Mixed vegetables (e.g., carrots, peas, bell peppers)

Olive oil

Onion

Garlic

Low-sodium vegetable broth

Salt and pepper

Preparation:

Rinse quinoa.

In olive oil, sauté the chopped onion and garlic.

Add quinoa and cook for a few minutes.

Add mixed vegetables and vegetable broth.

Instructions:

Simmer until the vegetables are soft and the quinoa is done.

Cooking Time: 20 minutes

Serving Size: 1 cup

Nutrition Value (approx. per serving):

Calories: 150

Protein: 5g

Carbohydrates: 30g

Fiber: 4g

Fat: 2g

Steamed Broccoli with Lemon

Ingredients:

Broccoli florets

Lemon juice

Olive oil

Salt and pepper

Preparation:

Steam broccoli until tender-crisp.

Drizzle with lemon juice and olive oil.

Season with salt and pepper.

Instructions:

Serve immediately.

Cooking Time: 5-7 minutes

Serving Size: 1 cup

Nutrition Value (approx. per serving):

Calories: 45

Protein: 3g

Carbohydrates: 8g

Fiber: 3g

Fat: 2g

Baked Sweet Potato Fries

Ingredients:

Sweet potatoes

Olive oil

Paprika

Salt and pepper

Preparation:

Cut sweet potatoes into fries.

Add paprika, olive oil, salt, and pepper and toss.

Arrange on a baking sheet.

Instructions:

Bake in the oven at 425°F (220°C) for 25-30 minutes, flipping once.

Cooking Time: 25-30 minutes

Serving Size: 1 cup

Nutrition Value (approx. per serving):

Calories: 120

Protein: 2g

Carbohydrates: 26g

Fiber: 4g

Fat: 2g

Brown Rice with Sautéed Mushrooms

Ingredients:

Brown rice

Olive oil

Sliced mushrooms

Onion

Garlic

Low-sodium vegetable broth

Salt and pepper

Preparation:

Cook brown rice according to package instructions.

Sauté sliced mushrooms, chopped onion, and garlic in olive oil.

Add cooked brown rice and vegetable broth.

Season with salt and pepper.

Instructions:

Sauté until everything is well combined and heated through.

Cooking Time: 30 minutes

Serving Size: 1 cup

Nutrition Value (approx. per serving):

Calories: 200

Protein: 5g

Carbohydrates: 40g

Fiber: 4g

Fat: 2g

Cucumber and Tomato Salad

Ingredients:

Cucumbers

Tomatoes

Red onion

Olive oil

Fresh lemon juice

Fresh basil leaves

Salt and pepper

Preparation:

Slice cucumbers, tomatoes, and red onion.

Toss in olive oil, lemon juice, fresh basil, salt, and pepper.

Instructions:

Before serving, let the food cool for at least half an hour in the refrigerator.

Serving Size: 1 cup

Nutrition Value (approx. per serving):

Calories: 60

Protein: 1g

Carbohydrates: 8g

Fiber: 2g

Fat: 3g

Ingredients:

Butternut squash

Onion

Carrots

Vegetable broth

Olive oil

Garlic

Nutmeg

Salt and pepper

Preparation:

In olive oil, sauté the chopped onion and garlic.

Add diced butternut squash and carrots.

After adding the veggie broth, bring it to a boil.

Simmer until vegetables are tender.

Purée the mixture until smooth.

Season with nutmeg, salt, and pepper.

Instructions:

Serve hot.

Cooking Time: 40 minutes

Serving Size: 1 cup

Nutrition Value (approx. per serving):

Calories: 100

Protein: 2g

Carbohydrates: 24g

Fiber: 4g

Fat: 1g

Creamy Coleslaw with Greek Yogurt Dressing

Ingredients:

Shredded cabbage

Shredded carrots

Greek yogurt

Dijon mustard

Apple cider vinegar

Honey

Salt and pepper

Preparation:

In a bowl, whisk together Greek yogurt, Dijon mustard, apple cider vinegar, honey, salt, and pepper.

Toss the dressing with shredded cabbage and carrots.

Instructions:

Before serving, let the food cool for at least an hour in the refrigerator.

Serving Size: 1 cup

Nutrition Value (approx. per serving):

Calories: 70

Protein: 3g

Carbohydrates: 10g

Fiber: 3g

Fat: 2g

Beet and Walnut Salad

Ingredients:

Beets

Walnuts

Feta cheese

Fresh basil leaves

Balsamic vinaigrette dressing

Salt and pepper

Preparation:

Roast or steam beets until tender, then peel and cube them.

Toast walnuts.

Toss beets, walnuts, crumbled feta cheese, and fresh basil leaves in balsamic vinaigrette dressing.

Season with salt and pepper.

Instructions:

Serve chilled.

Serving Size: 1 cup

Nutrition Value (approx. per serving):

Calories: 150

Protein: 4g

Carbohydrates: 12g

Fiber: 4g

Fat: 10g

Chapter 6

Overcoming Obstacles and Traps

Although controlling ADHD with food can be very successful, there are drawbacks and hazards to consider. For long-term success, it is essential to comprehend how to handle these difficulties.

Handling Withdrawal and Cravings

Making dietary adjustments for the management of ADHD can present a considerable challenge when it comes to cravings and withdrawal symptoms. Overcoming these obstacles requires the use of coping mechanisms and support networks.

Coping Mechanisms: Withdrawal and cravings can be severe, particularly if a high-sugar or processed-food diet was part of your prior diet. It is crucial to have a strategy in place in order to conquer urges. You can replace your favorite munchies with healthier options. For instance, choose fresh fruit or a tiny piece of dark chocolate if you're craving sweets. Exercising, like taking a quick stroll, can also assist in reducing cravings. You can also keep yourself on track by focusing on the advantages of your new diet and engaging in mindfulness exercises.

Support Systems: Establishing a robust support network is essential. Tell your loved ones about your nutritional objectives and how they may support you. Your success can be greatly impacted by having someone to confide in or keep you accountable when cravings occur.

Social Events and Eating Out

When adhering to a special diet for the management of ADHD, dining out and interacting with others can present challenges. Making educated decisions and communicating your dietary demands clearly are necessary.

Communicating Dietary Needs: Speaking with Restaurant Staff About Dietary Requirements: Don't be scared to let them know about your dietary requirements when dining out. A lot of restaurants are able to fulfill particular requests, such making dishes without specific components. Ask questions regarding the menu and politely let your service know what you need. If at all feasible, look up the restaurant's menu online to make a plan in advance. An enjoyable dining experience can be achieved by being explicit and forceful about your wants.

Making Informed Decisions: It may be tempting to stray from your ADHD-friendly diet while you're with people. Learn about healthier options and strategies to avoid this. Make dish selections that fit your diet. Think about packing a dish or snack that will satisfy your cravings without deviating from your diet plan if you're going to social events or parties.

Managing Emotional Eating

Emotional eating is frequently triggered by stress and other emotional factors and might interfere with your diet. It's critical to apply mindful eating practices and comprehend the relationship between emotional states and eating behaviors.

Stress and Emotional Triggers: The first step is to identify your emotional triggers. Emotional eating may be brought on by stress, anxiety, boredom, and other feelings. Once you've identified these triggers, you can focus on identifying more constructive coping mechanisms. This could involve methods for reducing stress including yoga, meditation, or deep breathing exercises.

Techniques for Mindful Eating: Mindful eating is the discipline of paying close attention to what you eat. It can help you avoid making impulsive emotional eating decisions. Concentrate on enjoying every bite and be mindful of the tastes and textures of your meal. Eat mindfully and without interruptions from TV or phones during your meal. By practicing mindful eating, you can avoid overeating by making smarter food choices and recognizing when you're genuinely full.

Managing these obstacles and traps is essential to keeping a diet that is conducive to ADHD. It's acceptable to seek professional advice from a dietitian or therapist, as they can offer tailored solutions for controlling cravings, emotional eating, and eating out without compromising your dietary objectives.

Chapter 7

Tracking and Evaluating Development

When you start an ADHD-friendly diet, it's critical to analyze your progress and make any required adjustments by keeping an eye on things. These are the main components of this procedure:

Recording Your Diet

Maintaining a food journal is an effective way to monitor your dietary decisions and how they affect your symptoms of ADHD. It can assist you in seeing trends and gaining understanding of how your nutrition impacts your overall health.

Monitoring Symptoms: Keep a journal of any adjustments or findings concerning your symptoms of ADHD. Take note of elements such as energy levels, mood, impulsivity, and focus. Provide as much information as you can, including the time of day the symptoms appear.

Discovering Patterns: Your food journal may show certain trends over time. You may see that changes in your symptoms are correlated with specific foods or food groups. For instance, you might discover that eating a lot of sugar increases impulsivity. Determining these trends will help you make well-informed dietary decisions.

Phase of Reintroduction

A critical stage in the nutritional journey is the reintroduction phase, where you progressively reintroduce items that you had previously removed in order to gauge their effect on your symptoms of ADHD.

Foods Should Be Reintroduced Gradually: Start by reintroducing one food at a time. Select a meal that you believe could influence your symptoms of ADHD. Reintroduce it into your diet gradually, starting with tiny amounts, and pay close attention to any changes in your symptoms.

Evaluating Reactions: Be patient and give each reintroduced item a few days to adequately assess its effects. As you reintroduce each food, keep a close eye on your symptoms in your food journal and take note of any noteworthy changes in behavior, focus, or mood.

Modifying Your Meal Plan

Your ability to make changes as needed will determine how well your ADHD-friendly diet works. To get the best results, you must adjust your food plan.

Optimizing Results: It may become clear which foods are helpful and which are harmful to your management of ADHD based on the observations you make in your food diary and your reactions during the reintroduction phase. Make the appropriate dietary changes. This could entail consuming more foods that promote your attention and wellbeing or removing particular trigger foods from your diet.

Consulting a Professional: A certified dietitian or other healthcare provider with expertise in nutrition and ADHD may be consulted in certain situations. They can offer professional advice and create a diet plan specifically tailored to your requirements.

Recall that following a diet that is conducive to ADHD is a very personal adventure. When tracking and evaluating your food choices, it's critical to be persistent and patient with yourself. You can use your food diary as a useful tool to help you make decisions about the foods that will best support managing your ADHD and your general health.

Chapter 8

The Extended Perspective

It's critical to keep the long term in mind when implementing an ADHD-friendly diet in order to have long-term success in controlling ADHD symptoms. This strategy includes a number of elements, such as hearing about success stories, taking lifestyle considerations into consideration, and maintaining and sustaining your dietary modifications.

Sustaining and Maintaining

Sustainability and upkeep are essential components of your long-term diet-based ADHD management strategy. These elements center on establishing a healthy diet and avoiding relapses.

Including Healthy Eating Habits: Your dietary adjustments should become more than a band-aid solution over time. Creating and maintaining better eating habits that complement your ADHD treatment plan is the aim. This involves incorporating wholesome decisions into your everyday schedule. Include in your diet a range of whole foods, fruits, vegetables, lean proteins, and whole grains. This will improve your general well-being in addition to helping you manage your ADHD.

Preventing Relapses: It's critical to hold onto the gains you've made. Continue to apply the techniques and tools that have assisted you in order to avoid reverting to previous eating patterns. Remind yourself of the beneficial effects your dietary adjustments have had on your symptoms of ADHD, lean on your support network, and go back over your food journal as needed.

ADHD and lifestyle factors

The management of ADHD is significantly influenced by lifestyle factors. This long-term strategy must include exercise, rest, stress reduction, and careful thought of supplements and prescription drugs.

Exercise, Sleep, and Stress Management:
Managing ADHD requires consistent physical activity, enough sleep, and skillful stress reduction. Include enjoyable exercise regimens, give a regular sleep pattern top priority, and engage in stress-relieving activities like yoga or meditation. The advantages of your diet that is conducive to ADHD can be enhanced by these lifestyle choices.

Considerations for Supplements and Medication: In certain circumstances, you may choose to combine your nutritional plan with supplements and medications. Seek advice from your healthcare professional regarding any prospective drugs or supplements that may improve the way you manage your ADHD.

Success Stories

Learning about the accomplishments of people who have taken comparable paths can inspire, uplift, and foster a feeling of camaraderie. Success stories frequently feature inspirational metamorphoses and first-hand accounts.

Real-Life Testimonials: Hearing from actual people about how they have managed their ADHD through nutrition can be comforting and inspiring. These testimonies can provide light on the struggles and victories faced by those traveling a comparable route.

Motivational Narratives: Accounts of people whose dietary adjustments have led to remarkable life changes can be quite effective in inspiring others. These anecdotes demonstrate the possibility of improvement and the practical benefits of an ADHD-friendly diet.

The long-term strategy for controlling ADHD via food is a thorough journey that includes sustainability, a holistic focus on lifestyle aspects, and drawing motivation from others' experiences. This method encourages both the treatment of symptoms associated with ADHD and the pursuit of a more balanced, healthier lifestyle.

Conclusion

In conclusion, embarking on an ADHD-friendly diet is a journey filled with hope, personalized nutrition, and the potential for positive change. Throughout this guide, we've explored the various facets of managing ADHD through dietary choices, from understanding the condition to implementing a personalized diet plan. We've delved into the essential elements of an ADHD-friendly diet, strategies for overcoming challenges, and the importance of monitoring your progress.

Summing It Up

The Power of Personalized Nutrition:

Your ADHD journey is unique to you. The power of personalized nutrition lies in the fact that what works best for one person may differ from another. Through careful observation, a food diary, and the reintroduction phase, you can tailor your diet to optimize your ADHD management.

Hope for ADHD Management:

The journey of managing ADHD through diet is filled with hope. By making informed, mindful choices about what you eat, you have the potential to positively impact your focus, mood, and overall well-being.

Your ADHD Journey Continues

Staying Informed and Updated:

Your ADHD journey doesn't end with this guide. Staying informed and updated about the latest developments in ADHD management is crucial. New research and insights are continually emerging, and it's essential to remain open to evolving strategies and recommendations.

Future Developments in ADHD Management:

The field of ADHD management is a dynamic one, with ongoing research and advancements in understanding the condition and how nutrition can play a pivotal role. As you move forward, keep an eye on future developments in ADHD management, including potential breakthroughs in dietary approaches and other complementary strategies.

Your journey to managing ADHD through diet is a path of empowerment and self-discovery. By combining the principles of personalized nutrition with hope, dedication, and a commitment to staying informed, you are equipped to navigate the challenges and embrace the opportunities that lie ahead. The power to enhance your well-being and effectively manage ADHD is in your hands, and your journey continues to unfold with each mindful choice you make.